A TEDDY BEAR'S
LITTLE INSTRUCTION
BOOK

Also available from Thorsons

A BABY'S LITTLE INSTRUCTION BOOK
David Brawn

A CAT'S LITTLE INSTRUCTION BOOK
Leigh W. Rutledge

A DOG'S LITTLE INSTRUCTION BOOK
David Brawn

THE DRIVER'S LITTLE INSTRUCTION BOOK
Mike Leonard

LIFE'S LITTLE INSTRUCTION BOOK
H. Jackson Brown Jr.

LIFE'S LITTLE INSTRUCTION BOOK, VOLUME II
H. Jackson Brown Jr.

THE LOVERS' LITTLE INSTRUCTION BOOK
Cindy Francis

THE PARENT'S LITTLE INSTRUCTION BOOK
Cindy Francis

A TEDDY BEAR'S LITTLE INSTRUCTION BOOK

David & Tracey Brawn

Thorsons
An Imprint of HarperCollins*Publishers*

Thorsons
An Imprint of HarperCollins*Publishers*
77–85 Fulham Palace Road,
Hammersmith, London W6 8JB

Published by Thorsons 1995
1 3 5 7 9 10 8 6 4 2

© David and Tracey Brawn 1995

David and Tracey Brawn assert the moral right
to be identified as the authors of this work

Illustrations by Caroline Della Porta

A catalogue record for this book
is available from the British Library

ISBN 0 7225 3214 8

Printed in Great Britain by
HarperCollinsManufacturing Glasgow

To the child that still resides
in everyone

Introduction

These days more than just a child's gift, Teddies change hands between collectors and between lovers almost as often as between sweet-smelling relatives and their newborn progeny. Some people will pay hundreds of pounds for a moth-eaten Bear stuffed with seriously old tights (or stockings, depending on its heritage). Others will acquire theirs much more cheaply, many making them for their families and friends (and themselves). Some

Bears are media stars and inspire commercialized copies. But – unless you're dragging a 1930s German original round the garden by its leg – the pedigree really does not matter.

Large or small, hard or soft, dressed or bare, Teddy Bears are Special. A shoulder to cry on, a best friend to confide in, a brave heart to take comfort from, Teddy is our companion through dark nights, cold winters, difficult journeys and family disputes. He shares our secrets, our picnics and our appointments with the doctor. And when he gets old and threadbare, he reminds us of when life was uncomplicated – and he is never too embarrassed to have just one more cuddle for old times' sake.

This book is designed to reawaken the child in us all, taking us back to the time when Teddy was best (or only) friend. It is also a book no self-respecting Bear, young or not so young, can afford to be without, reminding him how to behave, how to avoid abuse, and that he has a reputation to live up to.

Read it together and rediscover the true nature of Friendship.

A Note About Sex

We have used the pronoun 'he' as in our experience most Teddies *are* he-Bears. We recognize that there are of course many Bears who go by other less masculine names, and we therefore hope that all the Ms Bears out there will forgive us for such blatant sexism.

🐻 Practise a special glint in your eye when a child you like the look of enters your toyshop

🐻 Don't tolerate bear-faced cheek

- Get plenty of exercise – walk round and round the garden

- Eat up – obesity is more acceptable in a Bear than anorexia

- Only wear sweaters that fit

- Live to a ripe old age

- Have a 'dry clean only' label

- Don't be dropped from the pushchair

- Respect your elders – they're worth more than you!

- Never miss elevenses

🐻 If you lose a limb, a transplant will never look quite the same

🐻 Have an exciting job – be Super Ted's stunt double

🐻 Never be satisfied with the bear necessities

🐻 Don't eat sweets between meals

🐻 Never be used as a draught excluder

🐻 Be cherished – cultivate the 'cute' look

🐻 Travel in style – not hanging from the rear-view mirror

🐻 Don't become a projectile in domestic disputes

🐻 A Bear is for life, not just for Christmas

🐻 Be vegetarian – eat hunny and marmalade sandwiches

🐻 Rejuvenate your stuffing with a good massage

🐻 Don't sit on the windowsill in the summer in case you fade

- Save for the deposit on your first wendy house

- Hide behind the sofa when the monsters come on television

- Don't be judgemental

- Don't be a surrogate cushion

- Avoid banishment to the attic

🐻 When playing 'Doctors and Nurses', allow yourself to be bandaged, but not operated on

🐻 Never be a substitute handkerchief

🐻 Own up when you've been naughty

🐻 Be there when you're needed

🐻 Have a stiff joint and a loose one

 Don't take up a seat on public transport – sit on someone's lap

 Make sure Santa brings *you* a present too

- Have a secret name nobody knows about

- Visit a Teddy convention

🐻 Avoid the indignity of the Lost Property office

🐻 Be inscrutable

- Don't fall into the hands of a 'collector' who intends to keep you in a box forever

- Don't overtax your brain

🐻 If you find any loose threads, tuck them in – *DON'T* pull them!

🐻 Brighten up a dull room just by being there

If you have a wash:

1) Use an anti-dandruff shampoo
2) Don't shrink
3) Retain some dignity – be pegged up by the ears, not the feet

 On a farm trip, don't get too close to the animals (especially goats)

 Be cool – wear a T-shirt

 Don't ever change your gender

🐻 Don't be frightened if an Extra Terrestrial comes and hides in *your* cupboard

🐻 Make friends with everyone

🐻 Avoid getting tied to the bumper of a lorry

🐻 Eat plenty of fibre – include plenty of kapok in your diet

🐻 Form a jazz quartet and call yourselves 'The Forebears'

🐻 Forgive unfaithfulness committed by your owner towards other Bears

🐻 Never put off until tomorrow what you can cancel outright

🐻 Be environmentally friendly, but don't allow yourself to be recycled

Be a nature lover – watch the grass grow

If you're made of mohair, ponder on the nature of a mo

- Don't sit too close to the fire

- Ensure people honour your birthday

- Don't be a snob – be nice to pandas

🐻 Keep out of the way of the dog

🐻 Delegate the thinking to someone else

🐻 Remember, 'Hell hath no furry like a Teddy scorned'!

🐻 Play rough but fair

- Only ever fly in the hand luggage – never the hold

- Aspire to joining the Bear Force

 Don't worry if you're not part of a limited edition – *every* Bear is unique

 Don't let winning the National Lottery change your life

🐻 In a strange place, always take your bearings

🐻 Recall the old adage, 'Bruin is better than brawn'

🐻 Have your own passport and ask Immigration to stamp it for you

🐻 Avoid children who are eating chocolate or lollipops

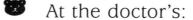 At the doctor's:

1) Share injections
2) Be in on the x-ray
3) Get the doctor to listen to you
   with the stethoscope

- In the office, get a human to do your typing – keyboards were *not* designed for paws

- Don't play in the snow without your scarf and hat

🐻 Listen to music – especially *Bear on a G-String*

🐻 Unwind – don't be a grizzly

Have eyes that follow people round the room

Wash behind your ears

🐻 Inspire political leaders – like Ted Heath and Tony Bear

🐻 Don't serve your porridge then go out for a walk

If you are a Highland Bear, sport your own tartan

Size is not important – small Bears can be just as expensive

- Be a team mascot

- Steer clear during potty training

- Examine yourself regularly for lumps

- Keep the right side of the fireguard

- Have a special outfit for weddings

- Go on a pilgrimage to Pooh Corner

Respect old Bears who insist on telling you stories about the War

Only give counselling if you're qualified

🐻 Remember, to be home-made is to be hand-crafted

🐻 Be photogenic, and always show your best side

 Be the subject of a still life art class, but don't be too sensitive about the results!

 Keep secrets

- Don't be uncouth – use a spoon when eating marmalade straight from the jar

- Follow fashion – don't be the Bear behind

🐻 If your owner leaves home, go too –
you can look after each other

🐻 Don't be part-exchanged for a
computer game

🐻 Enrol in a Bear club

🐻 Have your phone number written on your label so if you get lost you can be reunited

🐻 Hide under a dust sheet during DIY

🐻 Don't go near water if you have a growler

 Respect Bears of all colours and sexes

 Wear a hat to church

Some fashion tips:

1) Don't wear wellingtons that are too tight
2) Don't wear your duffle coat in the house
3) Don't wear yellow trousers unless you want to be labelled middle-class

- Don't feel too hurt when the time comes to sleep in your own bed

- Don't get involved in a tug of love

- Don't resort to cosmetic surgery except on medical grounds

Get a licence before you drive toy cars

Believe in the supernatural (but don't let on)

- Paws for thought

- Partake of a midnight snack

- Enjoy listening to scary stories

🐻 Have your own little seat on the back of the bicycle – and don't fall off!

🐻 Catch a cold the same time as your owner

🐻 Be proud if you have been in active service

🐻 Don't allow a ventriloquist to mistake you for a professional dummy

If your owner can't sew, seek out the nearest Teddy hospital

Wear your patches with pride

- If any parts of you are remotely dangerous, live on a high shelf

- Support a charity

- Have your photograph taken with the rest of the family for posterity

- Don't fight with the cat

- If you go to the supermarket, hold on tight

- Be a superhero in disguise

🐻 Have a President named after you

🐻 Be laid back – buy a hammock

🐻 Don't play with matches

🐻 Don't get on the wrong side of dogs
– they can be very destructive

🐻 Be a Bear of very little brain when
you need to be

🐻 Make sure you wear your wellies
before going puddle-jumping

🐻 Remember, the depth of puddles can
be very deceptive

- Dream of being a Teddynaut and blasting off to Ursa Minor

- Don't be arrogant – be gentle on a koala that thinks it's a Bear

- Never take the blame when you're innocent

- Learn self confidence – squeak for yourself

 Avoid puddles – inevitably they are followed by the washing machine

 Hand washing is much gentler than going in the washing machine

To avoid travel sickness:

1) Look out of the window
2) Play 'I spy with my little eye'
3) Stay at home

 Drip dry – avoid the tumble dryer at all costs

 Don't get stuck to the inside of a car window by four rubber suckers

🐻 Wear your armbands when swimming

🐻 Join 'Stuffing Watchers' when you are a little on the plump side

When camping, take only the bear essentials

If you have odd eyes, at least make sure they're level

-  Don't play war games

- Learn the history of your forebears

- After a stressful day, practise yoga

🐻 Stand out in a crowd

🐻 Even if you're off a production line, remember that *your* personality shows in your face

🐻 Don't be ashamed if you are stuffed with old tights

🐻 Have ambitions about being a footballer (not a football)

If you're unfortunate enough to be discarded, make friends with the dustmen

See the world – read an atlas

- Be discreet – hide your private parts from view

- Hold hands when crossing the road

🐻 Don't be shy – a shy Bear always gets left at the bottom of the toybox

🐻 Be calm in a crisis

 Teach your owner the words to the song so you can go picnicking together

 Never take part in drug smuggling

 Ensure you are indispensable, whatever the bribes to give you away may be

 Enjoy the classics – read Flaubear

- Be seen at night – don't go out in the dark

- If you have to be sent through the mail, insist on air holes in your box so you can breathe

- 🐻 Don't fall out of bed

- 🐻 Grin and bear it

- 🐻 A button in the ear is a sign of aristocracy

- Avoid taking sides in sibling disputes

- Don't get involved in pillow fights

- Be proud of your origins

- Bears are like chocolate – white, brown or plain, people love them all

- If you are a duty-free Teddy, take your travel sickness tablets

On holiday:

1) Sit on top of a big sandcastle
2) Wear a knotted handkerchief on your head
3) Stay up late

🐻 Don't sit on the stairs in case someone trips over you

🐻 Regenerate worn patches with a Bear restorer

Join the 'Bring Back Big Ted and Little Ted' campaign

Only be a scarecrow if the weather's fine

- Make someone's day – be a Teddy-o-gram

- Exchange photographs with a pen pal

- Espouse preventative medical care – don't get threadbear

- Audition for *Blockbusters* or *University Challenge*

🐻 Have a name people can spell –
unlike Aloysius

🐻 Be a gooseberry – get in the basket
with Andy Pandy and Looby-Loo

🐻 Ponder on why cats called 'Sooty' are always black, not yellow – is this flattery or satire?

🐻 Never bear a grudge

🐻 Do not practise acupuncture on yourself (unless you were designed as a pincushion)

🐻 Worship the sewing machine

🐻 Play safe – wear both team's colours at a football match

🐻 Be photographed for a book cover

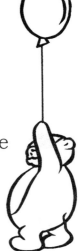

🐻 Be wary of an over-zealous arctophile

🐻 Play finger games – like, 'Round and Round the Garden, Like a Human Being. . .'

Start a race with, 'Ready, Teddy, Go!'

Don't be jealous of Yogi Bear –
his life was drawn out

🐻 You only discover your true friends when your honey pot is empty

🐻 Enjoy a good bedtime story

🐻 Be the unabashed subject of unconditional love

🐻 Read *A Teddy Bear's Little Instruction Book*

🐻 Scout for spiders before bedtime

🐻 Sit up straight

- Have a ferocious growler

- Have an eccentric side to your nature

- Join a hug

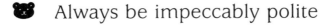 Always be impeccably polite

Wear designer gear if you go skiing

Sorry – bald Bears are *not* sexy!

- Don't sit in a draught

- Go bearfoot

- Marvel at rainbows

🐻 Be brave at the dentist's

🐻 Don't smoke (unless you're on fire)

🐻 Be smart – wear a waistcoat

🐻 Add to your value – cultivate a hump

🐻 Take part in bearobics

🐻 Don't go Absent WithOut Leave

🐻 Wear your seatbelt in the car

🐻 Don't stay out all night

🐻 Don't disclose your owner's age

- Live dangerously – parachute with a handkerchief

- Expect nothing – you won't be disappointed

- Be adventurous – accompany your owner to the toilet

- Don't get worried when people talk about riding bearback

It's a myth that the other Bear's honey is always sweeter

If you're a Polar Bear, don't pretend you're whiter than white

🐻 Read a magazine devoted to your kind

🐻 Have a smart yet untidy air about you

Regular health checks will keep you fit and well – check:

1) Stuffing pressure
2) Squeaker volume
3) Seam stresses

🐻 Don't go abseiling without a helmet

🐻 Never let a spouse come between you and your owner

🐻 Retire to a museum, not an attic

🐻 Go on a picnic every year

🐻 Be someone's best friend

🐻 Have an enigmatic smile

- Enjoy regular grooming

- Don't be a door stop

- Be a comfort during sad films on TV

Support a good cause:

1) Wear a bandage and help raise money for 'Children in Need'
2) Wear a poppy for Remembrance Sunday
3) But *avoid* red plastic noses – if the Great Bear had intended you to have a red nose, you'd be a reindeer!

 Help with the homework

 Have your own chair

 Model for paintings and sculptures

 Have your bumps read

- 🐻 Be the unsung hero of the hour

- 🐻 Come out of the closet

- 🐻 Grow old gracefully

- Lie in at the weekend

- Don't be used to wipe the windows

- Have a sympathetic ear

- 🐻 Take your medicine

- 🐻 Be brave – sleep with the light off

- 🐻 You're just stuffing – that's the bear bones of it!

Also by David Brawn

A BABY'S LITTLE INSTRUCTION BOOK

Never be seen in a frilly sunhat

Fill your nappy immediately it's been changed

Sneeze with your mouth full

Refuse to eat your dinner, yet have room for dessert

Be an angel at the childminder's and a monster at home

Stamp your feet when you can't get your own way

Disfigure your teddy bear with too much love

Also by David Brawn

A DOG'S LITTLE INSTRUCTION BOOK

Don't drink from a bowl with CAT on it

Keep your tail down when it's windy

Make friends with the local butcher

Never be seen in tartan

Don't eat slug pellets (or slugs)

Chase frisbees but not boomerangs

When you get old, learn some new tricks